**Looking
for Trouble**

Looking
for Trouble

Roque Dalton

Smokestack Books
1 Lake Terrace, Grewelthorpe, Ripon HG4 3BU
e-mail: info@smokestack-books.co.uk
www.smokestack-books.co.uk

ISBN 9780992958183

Smokestack Books is represented
by Inpress Ltd

'*A poet profound and cussed, preferring to take the piss than be taken seriously and in this way saved himself from solemnity, grandiloquence and other infirmities that have seriously afflicted Latin American political poetry. He couldn't save himself from his comrades. They punished his being different with the death penalty as if the crime of divergency was high treason. Dalton couldn't save himself from the bullet that came from his own side, the only one capable of finding him.*'
Eduardo Galeano

'*But above all else you
arrived early
too early
a death that wasn't yours
that at this time wouldn't know what to do
with
so much
life.*'
Mario Benedetti, 'For Roque'

'*For some years now I had decided to write fast, as if knowing that they'd kill me the next day.*'
Roque Dalton

Indice

Contents

Roque Dalton: an Introduction

'Cuando sepas que he muerto no pronuncies mi nombre
porque se detendría la muerte y el reposo…'

'When you learn that I've died don't speak my name
because then death and peace would have to wait'
                                        (Roque Dalton, 'Small Hours of the Night')

Published in 1962, the poem from which those words are drawn brings together, under one poetic roof, so many of the concerns that moved Roque Dalton in his life and work. He gave the poetry of his native El Salvador a fresh, modern voice, the voice of a restless and rapidly urbanising society chafing against the old order. He achieved a directness and intimacy in his poems that made him hugely influential in Latin American letters.

Yet in this poem's reference to death, we also sense the danger he faced as an urban guerrilla fighting for revolutionary change. Early death to Dalton was not merely a romantic trope, a sign of youthful angst. It was a possibility that he and thousands of other Latin Americans of his generation faced in their efforts to mobilise against the dictatorships that had settled on their countries like a black shadow. And in the poem's plea for silence, we see a stoic reminder of his years spent living underground, in the clandestine world of guerrilla cells, in which discretion was of utmost importance.

Roque Dalton was born in San Salvador on 14 May 1935, the illegitimate son of a Salvadoran nurse and a wealthy American sugar planter. He was raised in a working-class neighbourhood by his mother, who also ran a popular variety store where young Roque learned the popular, slang-laden language that later found its way into his writing. He attended a day school for the elite, the Jesuit-run Externado San José, paid for by his father. His life thus began with a series of acute contradictions, raised as he was in a poor neighbourhood yet schooled amongst the elite, disowned by his father yet subsidised by him. These ironies gave Dalton a sharp eye for the absurdity and hypocrisy of El Salvador's conservative order, which he spent his literary career holding up to ridicule and, later, sought to overturn with revolution.

In 1953, Dalton went to Chile to study law. Shortly after his return to El Salvador, the reformist government of President Jacobo Árbenzin Guatemala was overthrown in a CIA coup. Árbenz supporters streamed over the border into El Salvador, among them a young poet and journalist carrying a typewriter, Otto René Castillo. He and Dalton became close friends and collaborators.

In El Salvador, Castillo connected right away with a group of writers and artists who, from 1956, called themselves *la Generación Comprometida* (the Committed Generation). They shared a progressive outlook and a desire to open up the provincial and insular mores of Salvadoran society and, by extension, that of all Central America. Influenced by a Marxist view of history (although not all called themselves Marxists), they proposed a new understanding of their societiesthat eschewed the images of happy peasants and mestizo harmony and posited instead a history of ragged social conflicts, elite mediocrity and class violence. Castillo and Dalton together fired an opening salvo in the new poetic language with their book *Dospuñospor la tierra* (Two Fists for the Land) of 1955, a homage to two nineteenth-century indigenous martyrs whom they saw as precursors to modern-day revolutionaries.

Dalton, meanwhile, published his first important, solo book, *La ventana en el rostro* (The Window on the Face), in Mexico 1961. It was aslim volume of melancholy love poems and hymns written under the influence of Neruda. His work took a harder edge with his next book, *El turno delofendido* (The Offended Party's Turn), which, in an example of Dalton's provocative wit, was dedicated to the police chief responsible for his detention for illicit political activities in 1960. That detention might well have ended with Dalton's execution – many never made it out alive – but instead the military government was overthrown in a palace coup and Dalton was released with hundreds of other political prisoners. In 1964, he was arrested again in San

Salvador and this time had an even more improbable escape. While Dalton was in detention, an American CIA agent tried to recruit him. Dalton refused and was sent back to his cell, where, a few days later, he escaped by pushing through an adobe wall. This incident – recounted by Dalton in a posthumously published novel and confirmed much later in its basic outlines by declassified CIA documents – helped give him a reputation for miraculous saves and derring-do.

Dalton moved in 1965 to Czechoslovakia to take a job as a writer at the Spanish-language edition of *World Marxist Review*, a position that gave him plenty of time to work on his own books. After years on the run from police in San Salvador, his three years in Prague proved to be the most stable and productive of his career. In a modest Prague flat he shared with his wife Aída Cañas and their three sons, he wrote his most critically acclaimed book, *Taberna y otroslugares* (Tavern and Other Places), a blindingly original and self-confident volume of poetry, prose poems and theatrical dialogues that won the Casa de las Americas prize in 1969.

News of his friend, Otto Rene Castillo's death in 1967 while fighting in the guerrilla in Guatemala hit Dalton hard. Along with Che Guevara's death the same year, it likely contributed to his resolution to sacrifice a comfortable life in Prague and join the fast-brewing guerrilla struggle in El Salvador. He left Prague just weeks before Soviet tanks rolled in and headed to Cuba, where he lived until 1973, a period in which his reputation soared. At a time of shortages, uncertainty and relentless hostility from the north, Dalton's charming presence seemed to be everywhere in Havana: writing and producing a Brecht-inspired play with playwright Nina Serrano for Cuban television, writing essays for *Casa de las Americas* and *Pensamiento Crítico* magazines, holding forth at cultural forums. He wrote perhaps his most Salvadoran book, *Las historias prohibidas del pulgarcito* (The Banned Tales of Thumbelina), a collage of poems, anecdotes and news cuttings that showed the influence of his friend Eduardo Galeano. That book, its title taken from Chilean poet Gabriela Mistral's patronising reference to El Salvador as 'Thumbelina of the Americas', included the famous 'Poema de amor' (Love Poem), a warm-hearted paean to Salvadoran workers.

Yet Dalton's time in Cuba soon took a dark turn. He had a bitter falling out with the leadership of Casa de las Americas and saw several close friends lose their jobs during the revolution's early 1970s hardening. Friends in Havana said they lost all trace of him. They learned later he was completing an intensive guerrilla training course in preparation for his return to El Salvador. Many people seem to have had reservations about whether Dalton, inveterate drinker and bohemian now pushing forty, was suited to guerrilla life. But he insisted and so he went.

Dalton arrived in San Salvador in December 1973 for what turned out to be disastrous spell with a relatively new organisation called the People's Revolutionary Army. Hard-liners were in ascendancy. Some in their late teens and 20s, they knew or cared little about Dalton's career as a poet and saw him instead as a romantic, undisciplinedliability. He turned out one more book, a volume of poems written under five different pseudonyms entitled *Poemas clandestinos*, an act that seems to have alienated him further from the group's leadership. After a vicious power struggle, he was murdered by his own comrades along with another rebel, Armando Arteaga, in May 1975.

I first read Roque Dalton as an undergraduate at the University of Massachusetts in 1984 and have never been able to shake him off. I wish 'his monstrous death,' as Julio Cortázar called it, did not loom so large over his work, because his work was so full of wit, decency and compassion. Dalton reminded us of the responsibilities that we have toward each other and that writers do not live in a vacuum.'Poetry', he wrote, 'like bread, is for everyone'.

Roger Atwood

Como Tú

Yo como tú
amo el amor,
la vida,
el dulce encanto de las cosas
el paisaje celeste de los días de enero.

También mi sangre bulle
y río por los ojos
que han conocido el brote de las lágrimas.
Creo que el mundo es bello,
que la poesía es como el pan,
de todos.

Y que mis venas no terminan en mí,
sino en la sangre unánime
de los que luchan por la vida,
el amor,
las cosas,
el paisaje y el pan,
la poesía de todos.

Like You

I, like you,
love love,
life,
the sweet joy of things,
the heavenly landscape of January days.

Also my blood boils
and I laugh with my eyes
that have known the rush of tears.
I believe the world is beautiful,
that poetry, like bread, is there
for everyone.

And that my veins don't end in me
but in the common blood
of those battling for life,
love,
things,
the landscape and bread,
poetry for everyone.

Acta

En nombre de quienes lavan ropa ajena
(y expulsan de la blancura la mugre ajena)

En nombre de quienes cuidan hijos ajenos
(y venden su fuerza de trabajo
en forma de amor maternal y humillaciones)

En nombre de quienes habitan en vivienda ajena
(que ya no es vientre amable sino una tumba o cárcel)

En nombre de quienes comen mendrugos ajenos
(y aún los mastican con sentimiento de ladrón)

En nombre de quienes viven en un país ajeno
(las casas y las fábricas y los comercios
y las calles y las ciudades y los pueblos
y los ríos y los lagos y los volcanes y los montes
son siempre de otros
y por eso está allí la policía y la guardia
cuidándolos contra nosotros)

En nombre de quienes lo único que tienen
es hambre explotación enfermedades
sed de justicia y de agua
persecuciones condenas
soledad abandono opresión muerte

Yo acuso a la propiedad privada
de privarnos de todo.

Indictment

In the name of those who wash the clothes of others
(and expel from the whiteness others' dirt)

In the name of those who look after the children of others
(and sell their labour
in the form of maternal love and humiliations)

In the name of those who live in the homes of others
(because it's not a cosy womb but a grave or a jail)

In the name of those who eat the bread crusts of others
(and while chewing it feel like thieves)

In the name of those who live in a foreign country
(the houses and factories and shops
and the streets and the cities and towns
and the rivers and lakes and the volcanoes and the hills
always belong to others
and that's why the police and the guards are there,
protecting them from us)

In the name of those who only have
hunger exploitation illness
a thirst for justice and water
persecutions convictions
solitude abandonment oppression death

I accuse private property
of depriving us of everything.

Derechos Humanos

Recogido textualmente en una conferencia

— Hay negros en este cementerio?
—Enterrados no. Pero sí hay negros.
Los dos sepulteros son negros.

Human Rights

Overheard verbatim at a conference

— Are there any blacks in this cemetery?
— Not buried. But, yes there are blacks.
Both gravediggers are black.

Poema de Amor

Los que ampliaron el Canal de Panamá
(y fueron clasificados como 'silver roll' y no como 'gold roll')
los que repararon la flota del Pacífico en las bases de California,
los que se pudrieron en las cárceles de Guatemala,
México, Honduras, Nicaragua,
por ladrones, por contrabandistas, por estafadores, por
   hambrientos,
los siempre sospechosos de todo
('me permito remitirle al interfecto por esquinero sospechoso
y con el agravante de ser salvadoreño'),
los que llenaron los bares y los burdeles de todos los puertos
y capitales de la zona
('La Gruta Azul', 'El Calzoncito', 'Happyland'),
los sembradores de maíz en plena selva extranjera,
los reyes de la página roja,
los que nunca sabe nadie de dónde son,
los mejores artesanos del mundo,
los que fueron cosidos a balazos al cruzar la frontera,
los que murieron de paludismo,
o de las picadas del escorpión o la barba amarilla
en el infierno de las bananeras,
los que lloraron borrachos por el himno nacional
bajo el ciclón del Pacífico o la nieve del norte,
los arrimados, los mendigos, los marihuaneros,
los guanacos hijos de la gran puta,
los que apenitas pudieron regresar,
los que tuvieron un poco más de suerte,
los eternos indocumentados,
los hacelotodo, los vendelotodo, los comelotodo, los primeros en
   sacar el cuchillo,
los tristes más tristes del mundo,
mis compatriotas,
mis hermanos.

Poem of Love

The ones who died on the Panama Canal
(and were categorised as on the 'silver roll', not the 'gold roll'),
those who repaired the Pacific fleet in the bases of California,
those who rotted in jail in Guatemala, Mexico, Honduras,
    Nicaragua
for being thieves, smugglers, fraudsters, for being hungry,
those always suspected of everything
('Permit me to present this murder victim arrested for being a
    suspicious loiterer
with the aggravating circumstance of being Salvadoran'),
those who filled the bars and brothels of all the ports
and capitals in the region
(The Blue Cave, The Panties, Happyland),
those who sowed maize in foreign jungles,
the kings of the crime pages,
those who no one ever knows where they're from,
the best craftsmen in the world,
those who were mown down while crossing the border,
those who died of malaria
or scorpion or pit viper bites
in the hell of the banana plantations,
those who cry, drunk, on hearing the national anthem
under Pacific cyclones or in the snow-capped north,
the freeloaders, the beggars, the potheads,
the guanacos,* sons of bitches,
those who barely made it back,
those who were a bit luckier,
the eternal illegals,
the make-all, sell-all, eat-all, the first to pull a knife,
the saddest sad people in the world,
my countrymen,
my brothers.

Karl Marx

Desde los ojos nobles de león brillando al fondo de tus barbas
desde la humedad polvorienta en las bibliotecas mal alumbradas
desde los lácteos brazos de Jenny de Westfalia
desde los remolinos de la miseria en los exilios lentos y fríos
desde las cóleras en aquellas redacciones renanas llenas de humo
desde la fiebre como un pequeño mundo de luz en las noches sin fin
le corregiste la renca labor a Dios
tú oh gran culpable de la esperanza
oh responsable entre los responsables
de la felicidad que sigue caminando.

Karl Marx

From the noble, leonine eyes glittering from the depth of your beard
from the dust-laden dampness of the dimly-lit libraries
from the milky arms of Jenny of Westphalia
from the whirlwind of misery in the slow and freezing exiles
from the rages in those smoke-filled Rhineland newsrooms
from the fever, like a small world of light in the endless nights
you have corrected God's lame work
you, so guilty of giving us hope
oh responsible one among those responsible
for the happiness that keeps marching on.

Cristo

Crucificadle crucificadle
Crucificadle
porque a su tiempo más debido
no ahorcó a los señores del hartazgo
porque no dio cuchillos al genuflexo apóstol
porque repartió el agua de la humildad y el amor
en vez del ácido final
de la sedición.

Christ

Crucify him, crucify him,
crucify him
because when he should have
he didn't hang the men of greed,
because he didn't give knives to the servile apostle
because he shared out the waters of humility and love
instead of the fatal acid
of sedition.

Sobre el Negocio Bíblico

Dice la Biblia
que Cristo multiplicó para el pueblo
el pan y los peces.

Si lo hizo, hizo bien,
y eso lo hace mas grande que un gran general
que ganara mil batallas donde murieron millones de pobres.

Pero en la actualidad los norteamericanos
para evitar que el pan y los peces se multipliquen
y todo el mundo soporte con resignación
el hambre multiplicada que es parte del gran negocio,
multiplican la producción de Biblias
en todos los idiomas que hablamos los pobres
y nos las envian en manos de jóvenes rubios
que han sido minuciosamente adiestrados por sus Generales.

On Biblical Business

The Bible says
Christ multiplied for the people
bread and fishes.

If he did, he did well
and that makes him greater than a great general
who has won a thousand battles in which millions of the poor died.

But today the North Americans,
to ensure there is no multiplication of bread and fish,
and the whole world accepts it with resignation:
multiplied hunger that's part of big business
they multiply the production of Bibles
in every language we the poor speak
and send them to us in the hands of blond young men
who've been meticulously trained by their generals.

El Vecino

Tiene una esposa, más bien,
fea.

Tiene dos hijos que sacaron sus ojos
y que por estos días persiguen a los gatos en el barrio.

Trabaja, lee mucho, canta por las mañanas;
pregunta por la salud de las señoras;
es amigo del pan, el panadero;
suele beber
cerveza al mediodía;
conoce bien el fútbol, ama el mar,
desearía tener un automóvil,
asiste a los conciertos, tiene un perro pequeño,
ha vivido en Paris, escribió un libro – creo yo
que eran versos ,
se siente satisfecho al ver a los pájaros,
paga sus cuentas al fin del mes,
ayudó a reparar el campanario...

Ahora esta en la cárcel prisionero:
También es comunista, como dicen...

The Neighbour

He has a wife, rather,
ugly.

He has two sons who are the apple of his eye
and who these days chase cats around the neighbourhood.

He works, reads a lot and sings in the mornings;
asks old ladies as to their health;
likes bread and the baker;
usually drinks
beer at midday;
knows all about football, loves the sea,
wishes he had a car,
goes to concerts, has a small dog,
has lived in Paris, wrote a book – I think
they were verses –
he feels happy when he sees birds,
pays his bills at the end of the month,
helped repair the bell tower...

He's in jail now:
He's also a communist, so they say...

Recuerdo y Preguntas

Aquí en la Universidad
mientras escucho un discurso del rector
(en cada puerta hay policías grises
dando su aparte al la cultura),
asqueado hasta la palidez, recuerdo
la triste paz de mi pobreza natal,
la dulce lentitud con que se muere en mi pueblo.

Mi padre está esperando allá.
yo vine a estudiar
la arquitectura de la justicia,
la anatomía de la razón,
a buscar las respuestas
para el enorme desamparo y la sed.

Oh noche de luces falsas,
oropeles hechos de oscuridad:
hacia donde debo huir
que no sea mi propia alma,
el alma que quería ser bandera en el retorno
y que ahora quieren transformarme en trapo vil
en este templo de mercaderes?

Memory and Questions

Here at the university
while I listen to the rector's lecture
(at every door there are police in grey
lending support to the culture).
nauseous until I become pale, I remember
the sad peace of my native poverty,
the sweet lethargy with which one dies in my village

My father is waiting there.
I came to study
the architecture of justice,
the anatomy of reason,
looking for answers
for this enormous aridity and thirst.

Oh night of false lights,
tinsel made from darkness:
where should I flee
if not to my own soul,
the soul that wished to return as a banner
that now they want to transform into a shabby rag
in this temple of merchants?

Las Nuevas Escuelas

En la Grecia antigua
Aristóteles enseñaba filosofía a sus discípulos
mientras caminaban por un gran patio.
Por eso su escuela se llamaba 'de los peripatéticos'.
Los poetas combatientes
somos más peripatéticos que aquellos peripatéticos de Aristóteles
porque aprendemos la filosofía y la poesía del pueblo,
mientras caminamos
por las ciudades y las montañas de nuestro país.

The New Schools

In classical Greece
Aristoteles taught philosophy to his disciples
while walking around a large courtyard.
That's why his school was called 'the peripatetic one'.
We fighting poets
are more peripatetic than those Aristotelian peripatetic ones
because we learn philosophy and the poetry of the people,
while we walk
through the cities and the mountains of our country.

PR

¿Para qué debe servir
La poesía revolucionaria?

¿Para hacer poetas
o para hacer la revolución?

PR

What is
revolutionary poetry for?

To make poets
or to make revolution?

XVI Poema

Las leyes son para que las cumplan
los pobres.
Las leyes son hechas por los ricos
para poner un poco de orden a la explotación.
Los pobres son los únicos cumplidores de leyes de la historia.
Cuando los pobres hagan las leyes
ya no habrá ricos.

Poem XVI

Laws are made to be obeyed
by the poor.
Laws are made by the rich
to bring a little order to exploitation.
The poor are the only ones in history who abide by the law.
When the poor make laws
the rich will be no more.

Buscándome Líos

La noche de mi primera reunión de célula llovía
mi manera de chorrear fue muy aplaudida por cuatro
o cinco personajes del dominio de Goya
todo el mundo ahí parecía levemente aburrido
tal vez de la persecución y hasta de la tortura diariamente soñada.

Fundadores de confederaciones y de huelgas mostraban
cierta ronquera y me dijeron que debía
escoger un seudónimo
que me iba a tocar pagar cinco pesos al mes
que quedábamos en que todos los miércoles
y que cómo iban mis estudios
y que por hoy íbamos a leer un folleto de Lenin
y que no era necesario decir a cada momento camarada.

Cuando salimos no llovía más
mi madre me riñó por llegar tarde a casa.

Looking for Trouble

The night of my first party branch meeting it rained
my way of dripping was applauded by four
or five characters straight out of Goya's world
everyone there looked slightly bored
maybe of the persecution and even of the torture they dreamed of daily.

Founders of confederations and strikes revealing
a certain roughness told me that I had
to choose a pseudonym
that I had to pay five pesos a month
that we'd stick to meeting every Wednesday
and how was I getting on with my studies
and that today we were going to read a pamphlet by Lenin
and that we didn't need to say comrade all the time.

It had stopped raining by the time we finished
My mother scolded me for getting home late.

Misceláneas

Ironizar sobre el socialism
parece ser aquí un buen digestivo,
pero te juro que en mi país
primero hay que conseguirse la cena.

Para mí, el socialismo es aún una etapa burguesa
en la historia marxista de la humanidad. Y lo digo
precisamente en una mañana en que me reconozco
lúcido, cuando hace casi una semana que no pruebo
una gota de alcohol.

El imperialismo desea que la nación salvadoreña sea la Nación
Salvadoreña S.A., Made in USA.

Digan que somos lo que somos : un pueblo doloroso, un
pueblo analfabeto, desnutrido y sin embargo fuerte, porque
otro pueblo ya se habría muerto...

¿Sabe lo que sería El Salvador si fuera del tamaño de Brasil?

Miscellaneous

To be ironic about socialism
appears to be a good digestif around here
but I swear to you that in my country
you first have to obtain your supper.

For me, socialism is still a bourgeois stage
in the Marxist history of humanity. And I say this
precisely on a morning when I know
I am lucid, given that for almost a week I've not had
a drop of alcohol.

Imperialism wants the Salvadoran nation to become Salvadoran
Nation inc.,
Made in the USA.

Say what you will about us: a people suffering, an
illiterate people, malnourished and yet strong, because
any other people would have been dead by now...

Can you imagine what El Salvador would be if it were the size of
Brazil?

Vida, Oficios

Insoslayable para la vida,
la nueva vida me amanece: es un pequeño
sol con raíces que habré de regar mucho
e impulsar a que juegue
su propio ataque contra la cizaña.
Pequeño y pobre pan de la solidaridad,
bandera contra el frío, agua fresca para la sangre:
elementos maternos que no deben alejarse
del corazón.
Y contra la melancolía, la confianza; contra
la desesperación,
a voz del pueblo
vibrando en las ventanas de esta casa secreta.
escubrir,
descifrar,
articular,
poner en marcha:
viejos oficios de los libertadores y los mártires
que ahora son nuestras obligaciones
y que andan por allí contándonos los pasos:
del desayuno al sueño,
del sigilo en sigilo,
de acción en acción, de vida en vida.

Life, Occupations

Inescapable for life,
new life is dawning for me: it's a small
sun with roots that I'll have to water a lot
and encourage it to risk
its own assault on trouble.
The small and scanty bread of solidarity,
banner against the cold, fresh water for blood:
maternal elements which we can't alienate
from our hearts.
And against melancholy, trust; against
desperation,
the voice of the people
vibrating off the windows of this secret house.
Discover,
decipher,
articulate,
put in motion:
the old functions of the liberators and martyrs
that are now our own obligations
and that are out there counting our steps:
from breakfast to slumber,
from stealth to stealth
from action to action, from life to life.

Sobre Dolores de Cabeza

Es bello ser comunista,
aunque cause muchos dolores de cabeza.

Y es que el dolor de cabeza de los comunistas
se supone histórico, es decir
que no cede ante las tabletas analgésicas
sino sólo ante la realización del Paraíso en la tierra.
Así es la cosa.

Bajo el capitalismo nos duele la cabeza
y nos arrancan la cabeza.
En la lucha por la Revolución la cabeza es una bomba de
retardo.
En la construcción socialista planificamos el dolor de cabeza
lo cual no lo hace escasear, sino todo lo contrario.

El comunismo será, entre otras cosas,
una aspirina del tamaño del sol.

On Headaches

It is beautiful to be a communist,
although it causes many a headache.

You see the headache of communists
is supposed to be historical, that is to say
it does not respond to analgesic pills
but only to the achievement of an earthly paradise.
That's the way it is.

Under capitalism if our heads ache
they just take off our heads.
In the revolutionary struggle, our head is a time bomb.
In constructing socialism our headaches are pre-planned
which doesn't make them rarer, in fact the contrary

Communism will be, among other things,
an aspirin the size of the sun

Decires

'El marxismo-leninismo es una piedra
para romperle la cabeza al imperialismo
y a la burguesía.'

'No. El marxismo-leninismo es la goma elástica
 con que se arroja esa piedra.'

'No, no. El marxismo-leninismo es la idea
que mueve el brazo
que a su vez acciona la goma elástica
de la honda que arroja esa piedra.'

'El marxismo-leninismo es la espada
para cortar las manos del imperialismo.'

'Qué va! El marxismo-leninismo es la teoría
de hacerle la manicure al imperialismo
mientras se busca la oportunidad de amarrarle las manos.'

¿Qué voy a hacer si me he pasado la vida
leyendo el marxismo-leninismo
y al crecer olvidé
que tengo los bolsillos llenos de piedras
y una honda en el bolsillo de atrás
y que muy bien me podría conseguir una espada
y que no soportaría estar cinco minutos
en un Salón de Belleza?

Sayings

'Marxism-Leninism is a stone
to break the head of imperialism
and the bourgeoisie.'

'No. Marxism-Leninism is the catapult
with which that stone is flung.'

'No, no. Marxism-Leninism is the idea
that moves the arm
that pulls the elastic
of the sling that flings the stone.'

'Marxism-Leninism is the sword
to cut off the hands of imperialism.'

'Nonsense? Marxism-Leninism is the theory
of carrying out a manicure on imperialism
while looking for an opportunity to tie its hands.'

What am I doing if I go through life
reading about Marxism-Leninism
and on growing up I forgot
that I had pockets full of stones
and a catapult in my back pocket
and that I could easily get a sword
and that I couldn't stand even five minutes
in a beauty parlour?

Conversación Tensa

Qué hacer si sus peores enemigos
son infintamente mejores
que usted?

Eso no seria nada. El problema surge
cuando los mejores amigos
son perores que usted.

Lo peor es tener sólo enemigos.

No. Lo peor es tener sólo amigos.

Pero, quién es el enemigo?
Usted o sus enemigos?

Hasta la vista,
amigo.

Tense Conversation

What to do if your worst enemies
are infinitely better
than you?

That wouldn't mean anything. The problem arises
when your best friends
are worse than you.

The worst is to have only enemies.

No. The worst is to have only friends.

But, who is the enemy?
You or your enemies?

Till next time,
friend.

El Mar

a Tati, Meri, Margarita, con quienes compartí una ola…

I

Hay grandes piedras en tu oscuridad tempestuosa
grandes piedras con sus fechas lavadas por tu sombra
porque hasta el sol de día cómese tu sombra cruje
en el frío despidiéndose del aire que no se atreve a penetrarte.

Oh! mar donde los desesperados pueden dormir
arrullados por explosiones impasibles
alfabeto del vértigo paisaje diluido que los muros envisten
las gaviotas y la espuma de los peces son tu primavera
la furia es una pirámide verde
una resurrección del fuego más agudo tu clima
tu mejor huella sería un caracol
caminando con pasos de niño el desierto

(Amé siempre esas poblaciones disímiles
al parecer robadas de las manos del mar
pequeñas villas junto a la arena
puertos escandalosos en la ebriedad del salitre
caseríos tiritando entre la niebla llena de corales
grandes ciudades titánicas frente a las tempestades
humilladas aldeas de pescadores ciegos bajo un faro de aceite
factorías acechantes entre los manglares con un largo cuchillo

Valparaíso como una gran cascada en suspenso
Manta Puná puertos del Ecuador que me negaron las hojas
Buenaventura aromática como un gran puerto sucio
Panamá con los ojos punzados por la depravación
Cartagena siempre aguardando a los piratas hambrienta
Willemstadt náufraga en los dominios del petróleo
Tenerife y su dulce copa de vino
Barcelona bostezando entre los bancos y los carabineros

The Sea

for Tati, Meri, Margarita, with whom I shared a wave…

I

There are huge stones in your tempestuous darkness
huge stones with their dates washed by your shadow
because your creaking shadow eats even the daytime sun
in the cold, bidding farewell to the air that dares not enter you.

Ah! ocean where the desperate can sleep
lulled by indifferent explosions
alphabet of vertiginous watery landscape enveloped by walls
the gulls and the fish spray are your springtime
Fury is a pyramid of green
a resurrection of keenest fire your climate
your best spoor would be a snail
walking the desert with a child's steps

(I always loved these dissimilar villages
that seem stolen from the hands of the sea
small shacks strung along the sand
scandalous ports drunk on saltpeter
hamlets shivering in the coral-laden mist
vast titanic cities facing the storms,
humbled villages of blind fishermen beneath an oil-fuelled
lighthouse
trading posts lying in wait among the mangrove swamps with a
long knife

Valparaiso like an immense suspended waterfall
Manta Puná Ecuadorian ports that denied me their leaves
Buenaventura aromatic like a filthy big twat
Panama with its eyes stabbed by depravity
Cartagena, hungry, forever awaiting the pirates
Willemstadt shipwrecked on the power of oil
Tenerife and its sweet glass of wine
Barcelona yawning between banks and the armed police

Nápoles bellamente tumefacta
Génova Leningrado Sochi La Guaira Buenos Aires
Montevideo como una margarita
Puerto Limón Corinto
Acajutla en una lenta playa de mi patria
todos mirándose en el espejo grave que surcan los delfines
apartando
como un sable veloz las infinitas espigas de esmeralda.)

Naples finely tumescent
Genoa Leningrad Sochi La Guaira Buenos Aires
Montevideo like a daisy.
Puerto Limon Corinto
Acajutla on a slow beach of my country
everyone seeing themselves in the earnest mirror ploughed by
dolphins slicing, like a swishing sabre, the infinite spikes of emerald.

II

'*sal de los sacrificios*'
(García Lorca)

Si la noche rescata su cúpula de fósforo
y tus perdidos monstruos bajo el rayo se arrugan
los peces desatados son diez rápidos niños
que maduran profundos el himno de la escama

El oxígeno muerto sobre los minerales
cuando pasa un desfile de hipocampos dorados
enturbia el agua verde con su herida maldita
mientras prosigue sordo el rito de los pulpos.

Sal de los sacrificios vecindad corrosiva
luz sin fuego mordiente quemadura licuada
pálida sangre antigua de corriente furiosa
donde los ahogados resucitan su fiebre

El mar el mar entierra su salada noticia
el mar devora sordo la solar quemadura
el mar alza su rostro su cicatriz al cielo
el mar recae roto al cuido del abismo

En los embarcaderos nos engaña el aroma
de las algas vencidas de los peces amargos
el mar no es un cadáver es un sueño azotado
un móvil laberinto donde tiemblan los Astros

II

'salt of sacrifices'
(García Lorca)

If night rescues its dome of phosphorous
and your lost monsters shrink beneath the beam of light
the wild fish are ten fast children
who mature profoundly the hymn of fish scales

Dead oxygen over the minerals
when a parade of gilded seahorses passes by
muddying the green water with its cursed wound
while the deaf rite of the squids is resumed.

Salt of the corrosive neighbourhood sacrifices
light without gnawing fire scalding liquid
pallid ancient blood of a furious current
where the drowned resurrect their fever

the sea buries its salty news
the sea silently devours the solar fire
the sea raises its face its scar to the sky
the sea falls shattered into the care of the abyss

On the wharves we are deceived by the aroma
of seaweed defeated by the bitter fish
the sea is not a corpse it is a battered dream
a moving labyrinth in which the stars tremble.

ESTUARIO

Hoy has bajado desde el monte negro
otra vez sin tu lámpara.

(Vienes a mí en sigilo de dulce delincuente
evadiendo las miradas curiosas de la aldea
la envidia de las viejas hundidas en el calor
los gritos de los niños tratando de prenderse de tu frescura.)

Nos hemos quedado desnudos mirándonos en la suave oscuridad
recordando los viejos días que siempre renacen en la sangre
y a la hora de amar hemos sido tiernos como nunca
poblados de pequeñas palabras como nunca
todos nuestros sentidos abiertos como una flor al sol.

He despertado antes del amanecer
y veo que ha quedado la forma de tu cuerpo
retenida en la almohada.

Y he salido a lavarme con
el agua de la lluvia de anoche
y se me ha olvidado cantarle a las gaviotas
como todos los días…

ESTUARY

Today you came down from the black mountain
once again without your lamp.

(You come to me stealthily like a sweet miscreant
evading the inquisitive glances of the village
the envy of the old women sunken in the heat
the cries of children trying to capture your freshness.)

We stayed naked watching each other in the soft darkness
remembering the old days that are always reborn in blood
and at the time of making love we were more tender than ever
filled with small talk as never before
all of our senses open like a flower to the sun.

I awoke before dawn
and saw the shape of your body
retained by the pillow.

I went out to wash myself in the
water from last night's rain
and it made me forget to sing to the gulls
as I do everyday …

III

Un barco
cargado de tedio
un barco cargado de grupos taciturnos
escapando con muerta lentitud a las mandíbulas del sargazo.
En la proa cortamos el gran muro del aire
silenciosos estamos pensando en el país
donde el amor quedó temblando en su primera soledad.
Los libros están húmedos de sal
y el agua desde aquí parece una gran plaza desértica.
¡Qué jerarquía la de su soledad azotada!
¡La de su fría desnudez de piedra negra
que allá en el horizonte languidece en los brazos del viento!

III

A boat
laden with tedium
a boat loaded with taciturn groups
escaping with deathly sluggishness the mandibles of the Sargasso.
At the bow we cut the great wall of air
silent we are thinking of our country
where love remains shivering in its first solitude.
The books are damp with salt
and the water seems from here like a great deserted square.
What hierarchy in its battered solitude!
One of its cold nakedness of black stone
that languishes there on the horizon in the arms of the wind!

ESTUARIO

Ha terminado el amanecer de los nadadores.
No estoy comprometido.
Yo solamente abro la ventana
para que
os venga la gran rosa del yodo
la más diseminada la violenta rosa
que es aquí todo y en todo
establece su tacto.

Cuando os veo desnudos amándoos
bajo la leve sábana
-temblorosa mirada bajo los párpados cerrados-
Sé que no es sólo este mundo de borde marino
este filoso olor a sal caliente
lo que me enrostra las húmedas añoranzas.

Nunca debí dejarla ir.

Lo siento más en ciertos domingos como este domingo
once en que no os importa al final presencia
y copuláis largamente furiosamente bajo la leve sábana
temblorosa mirada bajo los párpados cerrados.

ESTUARY

The swimmers' dawn is over.
I'm not involved,
I just open the window
so that
the big iodine rose comes to you
the most scattered and violent rose
that is here everywhere and in everything
it leaves its touch.

When I see you naked, making love together
beneath the light sheet
– trembling glance beneath closed eyelids –
I know that it is not only this world at the sea's edge
this sharp smell of hot salt
that restrains my moist longings

I should have never let her leave.

I feel it more on certain Sundays like this one
the eleventh when my presence finally means nothing to you
and you copulate expansively
furiously beneath the light sheet
trembling glance under closed eyelids.

IV

El día en que el padre pez prolonga su castigo en el aire
el día en que se arriesga en el aire letal
prendidas a su última escama restos de algas
estos de pálidas algas amarillas
sobrevientes a no sé cuál sumergimiento
el día en que mi herida se detiene en la orilla de la espuma
al margen de su agresión diseminada de sus volátiles
dientecillos
el día en que la marisma es el horizonte
volcada en su ebriedad la rosa de los vientos
no se puede no se puede sino pensar
en los laberintos que debemos en los hondos secretos
que nos enmarañan el corazón.

Y no caben los exorcismos es el vacío pleno
el desasosiego en medio de la humedad ponderosa
todas las preguntas se van al fondo de los huesos
y ahí se quedan como las estaciones de año desgraciado.

Ni el sumum de las huellas podría amotinarse
a contrasombra se nos duerme la sed
y sólo la desnudez de las palomas resuena
en el oído que se confiesa hastiado de los golpes.

(Cómo quisiéramos ir hasta la raza de la clave hasta el murmullo
 seguro se sí mismo en la intimidad subterranean
¿pero cuál llave cuál cerrojo besar
que no nos venda a las facciones del guardian
con qué amargura echar toda la suerte que nos queda
sin que nos haga resbalar en sus traidores
vástagos resurgiendo de la ceniza?)

El mar y el momento son por ahora indescifrables.
Bebamos un vaso de este ron difamado
alejémonos hacia la altura de la playa
de este playa cuya arena es el cadáver de un mármol corrompido
y preparémonos para responder al sueño que vendrá.

IV

The day in which the father fish prolongs his punishment in the air
the day in which he takes a risk in the lethal air
attached to its last scale the remains of algae
those pale yellow algae
survivors of I don't know what submerging
the day my wound lingers at the edge of the foam
at the margin of its aggression scattered by its volatile
little teeth
the day when a swamp is the horizon
the rose of the winds toppled over drunk
one can't one can't but think
of the labyrinths that we have to carry in the secret depths
that entangle our heart.

The exorcisms won't fit inside the full emptiness
of unease in the midst of the ponderous wetness
all questions sink to the depth of the bones
and stay there like the seasons of a wretched year.

Not even the sum of all footsteps could rebel
in the counter-shade where our thirst falls asleep
and only the nakedness of the doves rings
in the ear that confesses it is weary of the blows.

(How we'd love to go to the keyhole to the whisper
so sure of itself in the subterranean intimacy
but which key which bolt to kiss
that won't betray us to the groups of warders?
with what bitterness to throw out all the luck we have left
without it making us slip on their treacherous
shoots emerging again from the ashes?)

The sea and the moment are indecipherable for now.
Let us drink a glass of this cheap rum
climb to the top of the dune
above the beach whose sand is a corpse of rotten marble
and prepare ourselves to respond to the dream that's coming.

En el Futuro

Cuando nuestra sociedad sea
básicamente justa
o sea
socialista,
en las conversaciones de las cervecerías
a la hora de las confesiones íntimas
más de alguno dirá, con la mirada baja
'yo tuve propiedad privada sobre los medios de producción'
como cuando hoy decimos
'yo tuve sífilis'
'yo tuve tendencias aberrantes en lo sexual

In the Future

When our society is
basically fair
that is
socialist,
in the conversations in the pubs
during the hour of intimate confessions
more than one will say, shame-facedly,
'I once privately owned the means of production'
as if today we would say
'I had syphilis'
'I had perverse sexual tendencies'

Hombre de Gran Ciudad

Dibújeseme la tormenta entre las manos
Para saciar esta diaria sed de estruendos
Como el caminante que se agacha a refrescar la suya de agua
En esas Fuentes que de la piedra brotan
Para vergüenza del polvo.

Big City Man

Let a storm arise between my hands
To quench this daily thirst for noise
like the wanderer who squats to quench his with water
from those springs that gush from the stone
to the embarrassment of the dust.

27 Años

Es una cosa seria
tener veintisiete años
en realidad es una
de las cosas más serias
en derredor se mueren los amigos
de la infancia ahogada
y empieza a dudar uno
de su inmortalidad.

27 Years

It's a serious thing
being twenty-seven years old
in fact it is one of
the most serious things around
to experience friends dying
and the drowning of childhood
and to begin to doubt
one's own immortality.

Por el Ojo de la Llave

Los mercados como un revuelto mar de grillos enemigos
Las manos de la desnuda estrujando la arena sin preguntar quién la
  cabalga
El pequeño coro de viejos fumando silenciosos ante el volcán dormido
Los ojos de los lagos sirviendo como casas a la luz
Los cementerios desperezándose al sol como gordos lagartos
Los niños panzudos en los barrios del lodo
Apedreando barquitos de papel y pájaros desde detrás de sus mocos
Los desocupados extendiendo la playa de piojos que tienen por camisa
Los homosexuales hurgando entre las piernas de los jóvenes
En los cines con olor a iglesia orinada
Los borrachos militantes de la desesperación
Lanzando el grito hediendo de hueca furia en medio de la noche
Los jirones del hambre que dejan los robafrutas
En las púas que guardan la tierra prisionera y la arboleda y el aire.

Through the Keyhole

The markets like a scrambled sea of enemy crickets
the naked girl's hands squeezing the sand without asking who rides her
the tiny choir of old men smoking silently in front of the sleeping
    volcano
the eyes of the lakes serving as houses of light
the cemeteries stretching themselves in the sun like fat lizards
children swollen-bellied in the barrios of mud
throwing stones at paper boats and birds from behind their snot
the unemployed extending the beach of lice that they wear as shirts
the homosexuals poking between the legs of the boys
in the cinemas with the stench of a urine-soaked church
the drunk militants of desperation
launching the stinking cry of hollow rage in the middle of the night
the shreds of hunger that leave the fruit-scrumpers
on the barbed wire that guards the imprisoned earth, the woodlands
    and the air.

Ya Ves Como...

desde Mexico, 1961

Ya ves cómo de todo lo que esperabas
Ayer en las tertulias de la Facultad
Sólo has venido a ser el gran amor del exiliado.

Tú que ibas irte con los príncipes
De fiesta por Europa que ibas heredar
A tres o cuatro viejos honorables
Tú la del coche envidiado y el traje de piel olorosa
Tú la de los grandes bazaletes de plata
Pero sobre todo tú la de los ojos más bellos
En toda la extensión de la ciudad
Ahora estás dormida
En los brazos del pobre solitario.

Yo veo la crucesita brillante en tu pecho
Mi retrato de Marx en la pared
Y creo que la vida a pesar de todo es bellísima.

Now You See How...

from Mexico, 1961

Now you see how of all your expectations
yesterday in the faculty lecture halls
you've only become the great love of an exile.

You who were going to walk with princes
partying around Europe you who were to inherit
three or four venerable old men
you envied for your car and your dress of fragrant leather
you of the huge silver bracelets
but above all else you with the most beautiful eyes
of anyone in the city
are now asleep
in the arms of a pitiful loner.

I see the shiny little crucifix on your breast
my picture of Marx on the wall
and despite everything I believe life is wonderful.

La Joie de Aimer

No me ames
para agotar tu destino.
No me ames
con la fe de construir una
tragedia contemporánea.
Ríete a todas luces, cariño.
Ríe en toda esta etapa de bella vecindad.
Ríete, ríete,
aunque sea de mí.

La Joie d'Aimer

Do not love me
to exhaust your destiny
do not love me
with the faith of constructing
a contemporary tragedy.
Laugh radiantly darling
laugh throughout this time of beautiful closeness.
Laugh, laugh,
even if it's at me.

Desnudez

Amo tu desnudez
porque desnuda me bebes con los poros,
como hace el agua
cuando entre sus paredes me sumerjo.

Tu desnudez derriba con su calor los límites,
me abre todas las puertas para que te adivine,
me toma de la mano como a un niño perdido
que en ti dejara quieta su edad y sus preguntas.

Tu piel dulce y salobre que respiro y que sorbo
pasa a ser mi universo, el credo que se nutre;
la aromática lámpara que alzo estando ciego
cuando junto a la sombras los deseos me ladran.

Cuando te me desnudas con los ojos cerrados
cabes en una copa vecina de mi lengua,
cabes entre mis manos como el pan necesario,
cabes bajo mi cuerpo más cabal que su sombra.

El día en que te mueras te enterraré desnuda
para que limpio sea tu reparto en la tierra,
para poder besarte la piel en los caminos,
trenzarte en cada río los cabellos dispersos.

El día en que te mueras te enterraré desnuda,
como cuando naciste de nuevo entre mis piernas.

Nakedness

I love your nakedness
because, naked, you drink me through your pores
like water does
when, between its walls, I submerge myself

Your nakedness breaks, with its heat, all bounds
It opens for me all the doors so that I may know you,
It takes me by the hand like a lost child
who in you quenches his age and his questions

Your soft and salty skin that I breath and sip
becomes my universe, the credo that nourishes me
The aromatic lamp that I raise being blind
when, together with the shadows, desires bark at me.

When you undress for me with your eyes closed
you fit in a cup next to my tongue
you fit between my hands like my daily bread
you fit beneath my body more neatly than its shadow

The day you die I'll bury you naked
so that you will be delivered clean to the earth
so that I can kiss your skin on the streets
and braid in every stream your unbound hair.

The day you die I will bury you naked
like the day you were born again between my legs.

El Olvido

Anoche soñé que me decían: tu amor ha muerto
Tu amor, la dulce amada de tu juventud,
ha muerto.

En una ciudad fría del Sur
donde los parques son una gran gota de rocío,
a la hora en que la niebla es aún virgen
y el cielo se rehúsa
a la mirada de los desesperados.

Y murió – me decían – sin pronunciar tu nombre.

Forgetting

Last night I dreamt they were telling me: your beloved has died
Your love, the sweet beloved of your youth,
has died.

In a cold city of the south
where the parks are a huge drop of dew,
at a time when the mist is still virginal
and the heavens spurn
the gaze of the desperate.

And she died – they said – without uttering your name.

Lo Que Falta

*'la otra persona, como persona, se ha convertido
en una necesidad pare él...'*
(Marx)

'Los clásicos son interesantes':
blasfemia mía de ayer, al salir de ver Romeo y Julieta.

Hoy aumentó la cuota de tomates para ensalada
y aparecieron unas acelgas enormes.

El pan sobra, los huevos alcanzan, el arroz y los frijoles
aburren como las cataratas.

La escasez da un poco de hambre mental
y muchísima de la otra, decía ayer el gordo Flores.

Pero con la merluza y dos bistecs
dejaremos atrás la semana.

Lo que verdaderamente falta en Cuba
eres tú.

What's Missing

'the other person, as a person, has become for him a need...'
(Marx)

'The classics are interesting':
a blasphemy of mine yesterday after seeing Romeo and Juliet.

Today the quota was increased for salad tomatoes
and enormous chards appeared.

There is plenty of bread, enough eggs, rice and beans;
they are as boring as waterfalls.

The shortages induce a bit of mental hunger
and a lot of the other, fatso Flores was saying yesterday.

But with hake and two steaks
we'll leave the week behind.

What is truly missing in Cuba
is you.

Canción Protesta

para Silvio (Rodríguez)

Cayó mortalmente herido de un machetazo en la guitarra
pero aún tuvo tiempo de sacar su mejor canción de la funda
y disparar con ella contra su asesino
que pareció momentáneamente desconcertado
llevándose los índices a los oídos
y pidiendo a gritos
que apagaran la luz.

Protest Song

for Silvio (Rodriguez)

He fell mortally wounded from a machete blow to the guitar
but he still had time to take his best song from the case
and fire it at his assassin
who appeared momentarily disconcerted
and putting his fingers in his ears
cried, begging
for the light to be turned off.

Poeta Libre

'Cuba sí, Yanquis tambien'
(Nicanor Parra)

¿Chile?
Depende…

Free Poet

'Cuba sí, Yankees also'
(Nicanor Parra)

Chile?
It depends…

Hitler Mazzini:
Comparacion entre Chile en 1974 y El Salvador en 1932

'No me extraña que calumnien
a la Honorable Junta Militar de Chile.
Los comunistas son así.
Dicen que en unos cuatro meses
los militares han matado
a más de ochenta mil chilenos.
Eso es una exageración
pues las pruebas concretas
dicen que los muertos no pasan
de unos cuarenta mil.
Así fue con lo de El Salvador en 1932.
Los comunistas dicen que el General Martínez
mató en menos de un mes
a más de treinta mil guanacos.
Eso es una exageración:
los muertos comprobados no pasaron de veinte mil.
Los demás
fueron considerados desaparecidos.'

Hitler Mazzini:
Comparison between Chile in 1974 and El Salvador in 1932

'It doesn't surprise me that they lie
about the honourable Chilean military junta.
Communists are like that.
They say that in about four months
the military has murdered
more than 80,000 Chileans.
This is an exaggeration
because concrete evidence
shows that there are no more than
around 40,000 dead.
As with El Salvador in 1932.
The communists said that General Martinez,
in less than a month, killed
more than 30,000 guanacos.
That's an exaggeration:
the dead, it was confirmed, amounted to no more than 20,000.
The others
are considered to have disappeared.'

General Martínez

Dicen que fue un buen Presidente
porque repartió casas baratas
a los salvadoreños que quedaron…

General Martínez

They say he was a good president
because he gave cheap houses
to the Salvadorans who were left...

La Certeza

sobre una idea de V.G.

Después de cuatro horas de tortura, el Apache y los otros
dos cuilios le acharon un balde de agua al reo para despertarlo
y le dijeron: ' Manda a decir el coronel que te van a dar un chance
de salvar la vida.

Si adivinás quién de nosotros tiene un ojo de vidrio, te dejaremos
de torturer.' Despues de pasear su Mirada sibre los rostros de sus
verdugos, el reo señaló a uno de ellos: 'El suyo. Su ojo derecho
es de vidrio.'

Y los cuilios asombrados dijeron: Te salvaste! Pero ¿cómo has
podido adivinarlo? Todos tus cheros fallaron, porque el ojo es
Americano, es decir, perfecto'.

'Muy sencillo – dijo el reo, sintiendo que le venía otra vez el
desmayo – fue el único ojo que no me miró con odio.'
Desde luego, lo siguieron torturando.

The Certainty

from an idea by V.G.

After four hours of torture, the Apache and the other two cops
threw a bucket of water over the prisoner to wake him up and
said: 'The colonel wants us to tell you he's going to give you
the chance to save your life.

If you guess which of us has a glass eye, we'll stop torturing
you.' After looking over the faces of his executioners he pointed
at one of them: 'Yours. Your right eye is glass.'

And the cops amazed said: 'You're saved! But how did you
guess? All your mates failed, because the eye is American,
which means it's perfect.'

'Quite simple,' said the prisoner, feeling he was about to faint
again, 'it was the only one that looked at me without hatred.'
Of course they continued to torture him.

Mala Noticia en un Pedazo de Periódico

Hoy cuando se me mueren los amigos
sólo mueren sus nombres.

¿Cómo aspirar, desde el violento pozo,
abarcar más que las tipografías,
resplandor de negruras delicadas
flechas hasta las íntimas memorias?

Sólo quien vive fuera de las cárceles
puede honrar los cadáveres,
lavarse del dolor de sus muertos con abrazos,
rascar con uña y lágrima las lápidas.

Los presos no; solamente silbamos
para que el eco acalle la noticia.

Bad News on a Scrap of Newspaper

These days when my friends die
only their names die.

How can one hope in this violent cesspit,
to take in more than the newsprint,
splendour of subtle blackness
arrows piercing even the intimate memories?

Only those who live outside the prisons
can honour the corpses,
wash off the sorrow of their dead with an embrace,
scratch the gravestones with their nails and tears.

We prisoners can't: we can only whistle
so that the echo silences the news.

Sobre Nuestra Moral Poetica

No confundir, somos poetas que escribimos
desde la clandestinidad en que vivimos.
No somos, pues, cómodos e impunes anonimistas:
de cara estamos contra el enemigo
y cabalgamos muy cerca de él, en la misma pista.
Y al sistema y a los hombres
que atacamos desde nuestra poesía
con nuestra vida les damos la oportunidad de que se cobren,
día tras día.

On our Poetic Morality

Don't be confused, we poets who write
from the clandestinity in which we live.
We aren't, then, idle, immune and anonymous:
we face the enemy head on
and we ride close to him, on the same trail.
And the system and the people
that we attack with our poetry
with our life we give them the opportunity of paying,
day after day.

Asesinado en la Calle

Desde tu corazón allanado por el plomo
¿no me darás la mano?

Desde tus ojos sordos donde ya no cabe la luna
¿no me darás la mano?

Desde tu derrumbada piel
¿no me darás la mano?

Desde tus venas asombradas por desembocar en el aire
¿no me darás la mano?

Desde la última palabra que pronunciaste – Carmen! –
¿no me darás la mano?

En la horrísona calle amotinada
Tu inmóvil muerte es la estatua de nuestra furia...

Assassinated in the Street

From your heart lined with lead
won't you give me your hand?

From your deaf eyes in which the moon no longer fits
won't you give me your hand?

From your shattered skin
won't give you me your hand?

From your veins shocked at disgorging into the air
won't give you me your hand?

From the last word you ever said – Carmen! –
won't give you me your hand?

In the dreadful insurgent street
your motionless death is the monument to our fury…

Monumento a la Vía Pacifica

Textual

'Nos oponemos rotundamente
a que se lleve al cabo el minute de silencio
propuesto en esta asamblea
en memoria del camarada Ernesto Guevara
Un héroe de su categoría merece
por lo menos media hora de silencio,
que es lo que nosotros proponemos desde esta tribuna.'

Monument to the Peaceful Road

as minuted

'We oppose categorically
that a minute of silence be observed,
as proposed at this meeting,
in memory of comrade Ernesto Guevara.
A hero of his standing deserves
at the very least half an hour of silence,
which is what we propose from this platform.'

Católicos y Comunistas en América Latina: Algunos Aspectos Actuales del Problema

A mí me expulsaron del Partido Comunista
mucho antes de que me excomulgaran
en la Iglesia Católica.

Eso no es nada:
a mí me excomulgaron en la Iglesia Católica
después que me expulsaron del Partido Comunista.

Puah!
A mí me expulsaron del Partido Comunista
porque me excomulgaron en la Iglesia Católica.

Catholics and Communists in Latin America: Some Aspects of the Problem

Me, I was expelled from the Communist Party
a long time before I was excommunicated
by the Catholic Church.

That's nothing:
Me, I was excommunicated by the Catholic Church
after I was expelled from the Communist Party.

Haha!
Me, I was expelled from the Communist Party
because the Catholic Church had excommunicated me.

La Cruz

¿De quién es ese extraño Dios?
¿Ése que ahora véndemos
rigurosamente medido?
¿Por qué desde su dura cruz
dicen que exige nuestro odio?
¿Por qué a su cielo único y solitario
no pueden subir nuestras bellas serpientes de colores
nuestros jóvenes embriagados
en la celebración de sus bodas secretas?

Ya con el látigo bastaba
Ya con el hambre el nudo que nos rompe
La furia del mosquete
Ya con la vehemencia de la espada
Buscándonos la raíz del aliento.

Pero tenían que llegar hasta el altar de piedra
Pisar el rostro de la fé que juramos
Al bosque en la primera lluvia de nuestra juventud.

Pero tenían que vencer a nuestros dulces dioses
Escupirlos vejarlos
Hundirlos en el lodo de la vergüenza
Abrir la desnudez de hierba y agua
De su infancia inmortal
A nuestros ojos torpes ya iniciados
Por las brilliantes baratijas
En la codicia ingénue del asombro.

The Cross

Whose strange god is this?
The one we now sell
meticulously calculated?
Why from his hard cross
do they say he demands our hatred?
Why can't they ascend to his one and only heaven
our beautifully coloured snakes
our young sons drunk
in celebration of his secret weddings?

It was already enough with the whip
and the knot of hunger that broke us
the fury of the musket
and the vehemence of the sword
searching for the source of our breath.

But they had to reach the stone altar
tread on the face of the faith that we swore
to the forest in the first downpour of our youth.

But they had to defeat our sweet gods
spit on them vex them
drown them in the mud of shame
open the nakedness of grass and water
of his immortal childhood
to our stupid eyes already initiated
by the shiny trinkets
in the naïve avarice of astonishment.

El Descanso del Guerrero

Los muertos están cada día más indóciles.

Antes era fácil con ellos:
les dábamos un cuello duro una flor
loábamos sus nombres en una larga lista:
que los recintos de la patria
que las sombras notables
que el mármol monstruoso.

El cadáver firmaba en pos de la memoria
iba de nuevo a filas
y marchaba al compás de nuestra vieja música.

Pero qué va
los muertos
son otros desde entonces.

Hoy se ponen irónicos
preguntan.

Me parece que caen en la cuenta
de ser cada vez más la mayoría!

The Warrior's Resting Place

The dead are becoming more restless every day.

They used to be easy
we'd give them a stiff collar a flower
praise their names on long lists:
on shrines in the motherland
of prominent shadows
in colossal marble.

The corpse signed away for posterity
came back to join up
and marched to the beat of our old music.

But what the hell
the dead
have changed since then.

They turn all ironic
ask questions.

It seems to me they've started to realise
that each time, they're becoming the majority!

Descubrimiento del Guernica

El toro impávido ante la lengua de los muertos
la muerte derramada bajo los cascos implacables
la impiedad del caballo entre el dolor de las lámparas
y el amor mío por el sueño
deslumbrado de pronto
por el remordimiento.

Discovery of Guernica

The bull, undaunted by the tongues of the dead
death spilled under implacable hooves
the cruelty of the horse between the pain of the lamps
and my love of sleep
dazzled suddenly
by remorse.

Soldado Desconocido

Quieren decir que la guerra es una gran malhumorada abstracta
con tus muñones de fuego fatuo y adivinación.

Pero mientras te regodeas bajo la bella montaña de piedra
bajo la nube de flores rígidas del homenaje
bajo el golpeteo lluvioso de los discursos
miles de soldados conocidos pasan cerca de ti cargando sus heridas
y dignamente te escupen.

Unknown Soldier

They want to say war is a great ill-humoured abstract
with its amputations of fatuous fire and divination.

But while you take pleasure under the lovely heap of stone
under the rigid flowers of homage
under the battering rain of the speeches
thousands of known soldiers pass close to you carrying their wounds
and with dignity spit on you

Él Pasa por una Fábrica

De México 1961

Mientras tiemble la piel bajo ásperas camisas
en el patio nocturno mojado por la huelga
toda la ferocidad del mundo se detiene con un cigarrillo
el amor es un ave perdida en el mar
sobreviviente de la tormenta del recuerdo

El viento bate las cejas de los viejos
habituados a ver agonizar el pan
mientras la miseria engorda sus telarañas
en los cuarterías cercanos que permanecen despiertos

Y yo me avergüenzo de ser el solitario
que simplemente sigue su camino en la noche
loando hasta hace un momento la tranquilidad
y hacienda planes para visitar Chapultepec
en la mañana de mañana domingo.

Passing a Factory

Mexico 1961

While the skin shivers under rough shirts
in the nocturnal yard drenched by the strike
all the ferocity of the world is paused with a cigarette
love is a bird lost at sea
survivor of storm-driven memories,

Wind whips the eyebrows of old men
used to watching the bread dying
while misery fattens its spider-webs
in the lodgings nearby that remain awake.

And I am ashamed of being a loner
who simply continues walking in the night,
until a moment ago, appreciating the tranquility
around him and making plans to visit Chapultepec
tomorrow, Sunday, in the morning.

Obrero Entrando a su Cuarto

Carbonizada la saliva tenue,
derramándose sobre su terror,
unos minutos antes en el sol de la calle, desconocido.

Oh, qué absurda es toda esta destrucción!

Día a día.

La telaraña es un puñal de polvoriento filo:
él comienza a toser
su sueño lleno de golpes.

Túnel truncado,
tumba de horrible chatura,
abismo tosco y breve.

Y lo peor es que la risa no rompa nada.

Las cosas no saben ni palabra del sudor,
del capataz,
de la humazón del horno que se pega a la piel...

A Worker Entering his Room

Charred is the faint saliva,
pouring itself over his terror,
unknown, only minutes earlier, in the sunlight on the street.

Ah! How absurd is all this destruction!

Day after day.

The spider's web is a dagger of dusty sharpness:
he begins to cough
his dream full of blows.

A tunnel cut short,
tomb of awful wretchedness,
a rough and brief abyss

The worst of it is that laughter breaks nothing.

Things know not a word about sweat,
about the foreman,
about the smoke from the furnace that sticks to his skin…

Dia de la Patria

Hoy fue el día de la patria: desperté a medio podrir, sobre el suelo húmedo e hiriente como la boca de un coyote muerto, entre los gases embriagadores de los himnos.

15 de septiembre

Independence Day

Today was Independence Day: I awoke feeling rotten, on the humid ground and hostile like the jaws of a dead coyote, among the intoxicating gases of anthems.

15 September

Santo Hernán

Hernán Cortés era un sifilítico iracundo
hediondo a cuero crudo en sus ratos de holganza
vengador de sus bubas
en cada astrónomo maya a quien mandó sacar los ojos.

Hombre hecho a las fatigas de los piojos
a los humores del vómito perla del agrio vino
ahora reposa entre los inconstantes brazos del incienso
bajo la misa diaria en la iglesia de Jesús Nazareno.

Saint Hernan

Hernán Cortés was a foul-tempered syphilitic,
obscene of body during his times of pleasure
avenging his abscesses
by ordering the gouging-out of the eyes of every Mayan astronomer.

A lice-ridden man,
governed by vomiting moods, brought on by the bitter wine,
he now rests in the fickle-armed embrace of incense,
under the daily mass in the Church of Jesus of Nazareth.

El Órgano de San José

for Luis Dominguez P

Vaso de la solemne tempestad,
de las arquitecturas de tu burbuja invadida
por las corolas de los astros,
del gran pilar repentino de las catedrales
nunca advertido por el ojo o la luz.

Acantilado de las agujas del gemido:
cambias en vino el huracán,
en gótica techumbre el espacio
donde nadan como niños loa pájaros,
en agitado temblor del corazon
el clima de la música.

Hermano de un dios bronco y anatema:
cuando callas dejas el suelo de la iglesia
lleno de negros cadáveres de rosas.

The Organic of St Joseph

for Luis Dominguez P

Glass of the solemn tempest
of the architectures of your bubble invaded
by corollas of stars,
of the great sudden columns of the cathedrals
never noticed by the eye or the light.

A cliff of wailing spires:
you change the hurricane into wine
in the gothic roofing the space
where birds swim like children
in the palpitation of the heart
the climate of music.

Brother of a hoarse god that is anathema:
when you remain silent you leave the floor of the church
full of black corpses of roses.

Dos Guerrilleros Griegos:
un Viejo y un Traidor

a la memoria de Nikos Kazantzakis

Panayotaros nunca le puso rosas al fusil.

A sus prímeras victimas en las emboscadas
se negó enterrar como era la costumbre:
las dejó para siempre hurfanas de la cruz
mientras el duro sol reía afilando sus garras.

Entonces habia harto vino ácido y queso sustancial
y por la noches Demetrio el panadero
tocaba para bailes grotescos
su pequeña guitarra.

Panayotaros se fue cuando nos vino el hambre
y hasta las culebras llegaban a morir cerca de nuestros pies.

Ahora será ministro o algo así
a juzgar por el respeto con que pronuncian su nombre
todos los medicos en este hospital horrible de olvidados…

Two Greek Guerrillas:
an Old Man and a Traitor

in memory of Nikos Kazantzakis

Panayotaros never put roses in the barrel of his gun.

The first victims of his ambushes
he refused to bury as was customary:
leaving them forever orphans of the cross
while the harsh sun laughed sharpening its claws.

In those days bitter wine and rich cheese were plentiful
at night Demetrios the baker
played for grotesque dances
on his small guitar.

Panayotaros left when hunger came to us
and even the snakes would die at our feet.

He'll be a minister or some such thing now
to judge by the respect with which his name is uttered
by all the doctors in this terrible hospital of the forgotten...

Mis Militares III – Los H.P. (Hijos Pródigos)

Los soldados ingleses mataron
chipriotas,
árabes,
tanganikenses,
georgianos,
persas,
hindúes,
pakistanos,
chinos,
turcos,
polinesios.
Los soldados ingleses hoy matan
irlandeses.
Así retorna el tigre al hogar,
a la cultura cristiana,
a la civilización occidental.
Así hermana el tigre a los hombres:
en la patria, en la cultura de la muerte.

My Military III – the P.S. (prodigal sons)

English soldiers killed
Cypriots
Arabs
Tanganyikans
Georgians
Persians
Hindus
Pakistanis
Chinese
Turks
Polynesians.
English soldiers today kill
Irishmen.
So, now the tiger returns home,
to its Christian culture,
to Western culture.
That's how the tiger unites people:
in the motherland, in the culture of death.

Izalco

El volcán apagado gran herida
De sombra presa entre las hondas piedras
Gran borbollón de noches
Al pie del preso por el sol
Presa derrota de la Madre Tierra
Que les deja su cólera a los hombres

Izalco

The volcano a vast extinguished wound
of captured shadow between deep rocks
great cauldron of nights
at the foot of the sun's prisoner
defeated captive of mother Earth
that leaves them its rage at humankind.

Paráble a Partir de la Vulcanología Revisionista

El volcán de Izalco,
Como volcán,
Era ultraizquierdista.

Echaba lava y piedras por la boca
Y hacía ruido y hacía temblar,
Atentando contra la paz y la tranquilidad.

Hoy es un buen volcán civilizado
Que coexistirá pacíficamente
Con el Hotel de Montaña del Cerro Verde
Y al cual podremos ponerle en el hocico
Fuegos artificiales como los que echan
Los diputados populares.

Vocán para ejecutivos
Y hasta revolucionarios y sindicalistas
Que saben quedarse en su lugar y no son celenturientos,
Ya no sera el símbolo de los locos tonantes guerrilleristas
Que son los unicos que añoran sus ex-abruptos geológicos.

Proletarios repetables y mansos del mundo,
El Comité Central os invita
A aprender la lección que da el volcán de Izalco:
El fuego a pasado de moda,
¿por qué habremos entonces de querer llevarlo nosotros
dentro del corazón?

A Parable Based on Revisionist Volcanology

The Izalco volcano,
as a volcano
was ultra-leftist.

It spewed lava and rocks from its mouth
and made rumbles and tremors,
threatening peace and tranquility.

Today it is a good volcano, civilised,
that will coexist peacefully
with the Cerro Verde Mountain Hotel
and in whose gob we can put
fireworks of the sort thrown
by the people's representatives.

A volcano for executives
and even for revolutionaries and trade unionists
who know their place and don't get agitated
It won't be a symbol anymore of mad thunderous guerrilleristas
who are the only ones who yearn for its past geological eruptions.

Respectable and docile proletarians of the world
the Central Committee invites you
to learn the lesson of the Izalco volcano:
fire is no longer trendy,
so why would we want to still carry it
in our hearts?

Para Cuando la Muerte...

Para cuando la muerte con sus pájaros
De espuma negra brote de mi piel
Para cuando mis huesos interroguen
Al aire por sus jugos y mareas
Y del ojo caido las raíces
Eleven sus rituals desolados
Para cuando ya sea el substituido
Por los caminos el único que falta
Para cerrar la cuenta de los pasos del día
Mis palabras ahogadas seguirán animando
En tu cuerpo de plata la cosecha Madura

Al olvido tenaces le dimos muerte complete
Viajeros de la misma religion amorosa.

Until Death…

Until death with its birds
of black froth sprouts from my skin
Until my bones interrogate
the air for its juices and tides
and from the fallen eye the roots
lift their desolate rituals
Until I become the replacement
for the paths the only one missing
in order to complete the story of the day's steps
my drowned words will continue encouraging
the ripe harvest in your body of silver

We killed tenacious oblivion completely
travellers of the same loving religion.

Murió Mariano el Músico.

Donde esperaba el piano ya no hay pájaros
sólo vagos recuerdos de un temblor innombrable.

El polvo cae ahora totalmente
Sin hallar a su paso la estatura del ébano.

La puerta del jardín no se abre más.

A veces pienso si no sufren tanto
como las viudas
las habitaciones que dejamos al morir.

Al menos cuando uno ha cantado
o hecho música dulce,
como Mariano, en ellas…

Mariano the Musician has Died...

Where the piano waited there are no longer any birds
only vague memories of an unnamed tremor.

The dust falls now completely
without finding the statue of ebony in its way.

The door to the garden doesn't get opened any more.

At times I wonder if they don't suffer
like the widows
those rooms we leave when we die.

At least when someone has sung
or made sweet music
in them, as Mariano did ...

Notes

Poema de Amor/Poem of Love
Guanaco is a type of llama as well as an affectionate term for Salvadorans.

Canción Protesta/Protest Song
Silvio Rodríguez is one of Cuba's best loved singers.Author of highly poetic lyrics with a hard political edge whose songs are classics of Latin American music such as Ojalá, Playa Girón, Unicornio and La Maza. He has nearly 20 albums to his name.

General Martínez
General Martinez was the president of El Salvador from 1931 to 1944. While he was serving as President Arturo Araujo's vice-president and defense minister, a directorate seized power during a palace coup. He brutally suppressed all opposition, particularly the Salvadoran peasant revolt of 1932 led by Farabundo Martí, when thousands of people were massacred if they were suspected of collaboration with the communists. It became known as La Matanza. The specific number of victims is unknown but estimates range from 10,000 to 40,000

Dos Guerrilleros Griegos/Two Greek Guerrillas
Nikos Kazantzakis is Crete's most renowned revolutionary author.

Izalco
The Izalco is on the side of the Santa Ana Volcano, in western El Salvador. It erupted almost continuously from 1770 (when it formed) to 195,8 earning the nickname of 'Lighthouse of the Pacific'. In Antoine de Saint-Exupéry's Le Petit Prince, the Prince's Asteroid has three minuscule volcanoes, one of which is called Izalco, a nod to the author's Salvadoran wife Consuelo. The volcano in Latin America is also a traditional symbol of rebellion and revolution.

Our thanks are due to Roger Atwood, an acknowledged authority on the writings of Roque Dalton, for writing the introduction to this selection and for his expert advice and generous help on the project, also to Werner Matias Romero, former ambassador for El Salvador in London, and last but not least to Roque Dalton's sons – Juan José y Jorge Dalton for their help and support for this project. We were also inspired and stimulated by the full-length documentary, *Roque Dalton – Let's Shoot the Night* (2014), directed by Tina Leisch.

Translating literature always involves a large dose of subjectivity and personal preference; poetry is particularly prone to this tendency. However, in these translations we have endeavoured to stay as close as possible to the original Spanish word order, rhythm and syntax where possible; we have avoided the temptation of smoothing, simplifying or over-interpreting. As so often with translations, even though all those in this volume are our own, they owe much to other translators – in the main North American – who led the way in making the works of Dalton available to an English-speaking readership. However, in our translations we have adhered to British English throughout. As source material we have used the volumes: *No Pronuncies Mi Nombre, Poesía Completa de Roque Dalton* (3 vols). Published by Direccíon de Publicaciones e Impresos (DPI), Consejo Nacional para la Cultura y el Arte (Concultura), San Salvador 2005, reprinted 2009.

Dalton, in his poetry, was in many ways a child of the Chilean poet Nicanor Parra whose 'antipoems' changed the language of poetry in Latin America. Parra was emblematic of a generational change when the manner, vocabulary and imagery of popular speech was incorporated lock, stock and barrel into poetry, as was irony and banter. His poetry represented a tectonic shift that went hand in hand with the articulation of socialist ideas of liberation. Dalton took up and developed that tradition in his own inimitable way. He was very much a poetic innovator, creating pithy poems from everyday incidents; he could be ironic, satirical and humorous. He uses the street language of his native El Salvador to convey the raw earthiness of life.

Michal Boncza was born in the UK, spent his childhood in Argentina and his youth in Poland where he studied architecture. He is a journalist, graphic designer and translator, specialising in translations from the Spanish. He currently works at the *Morning Star* newspaper. Together they edited and translated *The Arrival of the Orchestra* by the Venezuelan poet Gustavo Pereira (also published by Smokestack).

John Green was a documentary film maker for twenty years, covering social and political issues throughout the world for GDR television. His books include *Engels: A Revolutionary Life*, *Ken Sprague: People's Artist, Red Reporter* and (with Bruni de la Motte) *Stasi Hell or Workers' Paradise: Socialism in the German Democratic Republic.* Many of his translations of Victor Jara were included in *His Hands Were Gentle: Selected Lyrics of Victor Jara* (also published by Smokestack).

Roger Atwood teaches at the University of the District of Columbia in Washington and writes regularly for *The Times Literary Supplement.* His essays on Roque Dalton are widely published, including in *Latin American Research Review*, *Realidad* and *El Faro*.